Instant Omni Pro Air Fryer Oven Combo Cookbook for Beginners

1000-Day Crispy and Easy Recipes for Your Instant Omni Pro Air Fryer Oven Combo to Fry, Bake, Grill & Roast and More

Trein Yean

Table of contents

Introduction

Do you have an Instant Omni Pro Air Fryer Oven Combo but don't know how to use? This best-selling Instant Omni Pro Air Fryer Oven Combo cookbook will teach you how to start and also including lots of healthy recipes. You can search for recipes by cuisine, preparation time, meal type, etc. I believe that you will get satisfied advice that suits your taste and eating habits from this cookbook.

Science tells us that air fried foods are a healthier alternative to traditionally fried foods. Cooking with air instead of oil is better for your health and shopping budget and offers tons of benefits like improving your appetite, cholesterol, blood pressure and reversing diabetes. With this cookbook you will become a richer, happier and healthier cook in no time!

This book is written for all those beginners who do not know how to use a Instant Omni Pro Air Fryer Oven Combo or advanced users who want to try new and tasty recipes. Inside, you'll love a tasty variety of savory, salty, crispy and delicious meals, as well as a wonderful selection of traditional and modern recipes

Chapter 1: Understanding Instant Omni Pro Air Fryer Oven Combo

The Instant Omni Pro Air Fryer Oven Combo is the perfect oven to use in the home kitchen or in a professional setting. Whether you are an expert or a beginner, its range of cooking programs, and easy to use control panel will definitely make cooking a convenient job for you. This toaster oven is a breeze for those who want to cook large servings at a time. It is an advanced version of the previously launched Instant Omni, and it provides greater capacity and additional cooking functions.

Advantages of Using Instant Omni

The following features of the Instant Omni make this toaster a must to keep cooking appliance:

1. **Eight Smart functions**

This toaster oven combines all the cooking functions of an oven, broiler, air fryer, and a toaster. Imagine you have one single appliance that can carry out all such functions. Each smart program comes with a preset temperature and timer settings, which are also adjustable as per the needs. The seven cooking programs of the Instant Omni toaster oven includes:

- Air Fry
- Broil
- Bake
- Roast
- Toast
- Dehydrate
- Slow Cook
- Reheat

2. **Two cooking modes**

One feature that makes Instant Omni a toaster oven different from other toaster ovens is its two cooking modes. This feature is rare or impossible to find in other toaster ovens. There are two cooking modes which can be used to cook different types of meals. The two modes are:

- **Rotate**

Using this mode, a user can cook or roast its chicken, duck, or any other meat on the rotisserie. The heat is provided to the food as it rotates on the rotisserie stick.

- **Convection**

This mode is suitable for all other cooking functions in which food is placed in a fixed position. The heat is produced and regulated inside the oven through convection.

3. XL Capacity

The size of Instant Omni takes it to the top of the list when compared to other toaster ovens. Its great capacity to accommodate all food types, whether you want to cook a whole chicken inside or what to Air fryer a large batch of French fries, the appliance is capable of carrying them all at a time. So, it is perfect to use for large families. The XL capacity of the Instant Omni can cook the following in a single layer:

- 12" Pizza
- Six Toast Slices

4. Easy to Read Display screen

The display panel of the Instant Omni is easy to understand. It has a display at the center, which is surrounded by the touch keys for all the smart programs, the cooking modes, and the on/off functions. There are separate knobs attached at the two ends of the touch panel, which can be used to adjust the cooking programs, time, and temperature manually.

5. Intuitive Customizable Programs

All the smart programs of Instant Omni are customizable. Even when the cooking program is running, the settings can be changed using the temperature and time knobs. The adjustable programs allow the users to switch from one cooking settings to another with its super flexible heating system.

6. Even-Heat: Toasts Both Sides

Due to its convection heating mechanism, the Instant Omni toaster oven is capable of heating the food from all sides. This feature ensures even heating. When bread slices or bagels are toasted inside this toaster oven, they are cooked both from the top and the bottom. Without flipping a single slice, a user can get evenly cooked and crispy toasts.

Unboxing the Instant Omni Pro Air Fryer Oven Combo

When it comes to electric appliances, it is important to inspect all the parts of the appliance before giving it a test run. The Instant Omni toaster oven comes with the following basic elements and the accessories.

- The Oven Base unit
- Rack tray
- Crumb Tray
- Oven Door
- Rotisserie Catch
- Rotisserie Spit & Forks Rotisserie Lift
- Air Fry Basket
- Baking pan
- Baking trays
- Power plug

Inside the Instant Omni plus oven, there are three grooves on both sides. These grooves are used to insert three rack trays in the oven. The uppermost grooves can be used to insert the trays when the food needs to be broiled. The center grooves are for Air frying and Roasting purposes. The lowermost level is used to place the food which needs to be baked, reheated, or dehydrated. Crumb tray is inserted at the bottom to protect the bottom of the oven from the food particle during cooking. The rotisserie stick can be inserted and used to fix the meat of chicken. This stick can be fixed on the inner side of the center portion of the oven into the rotisserie catch. Air fryer basket can be placed on the lower rack when required.

Control Panel

The control panel of the appliance is fixed on the front top portion of the oven. The center black panel consists of the touch screen, which shows all the functions. This panel is placed in between two knobs which are used to adjust the time and cooking temperature:

- Smart Program Keys: The seven smart program keys are located at the bottom of the black panel. Any of the programs can be selected by rotating the preset dial.
- Display: right above the keys, there is a display which lights in blue colored figures indicating the time, temperature, and other indicators like Start, Cancel, Door, Warm, Flip or turn, etc.
- Cooking Modes: There are two keys to the cooking modes, indicated by the: Rotate and Convection marks.
- Start and Cancel Key: At the two corners of the display screen, there are keys to start or cancel a selected program.
- Dials: The Temp/time dial can be used to adjust the cooking time and temperature. Rotate the dial to the right to increase the value of rotate it to the left to decrease the values. The Preset dial is used to switch the cooking modes.

Featured Cooking Functions and Programs

There are eight smart programs that give different cooking modes to the users, which are as follow:

1. **Air Fry**

Using this program, to cook oil-free, crispy food, whether its coated meat or fries, everything can be fried in its Air fryer basket.

2. **Toast**

The temp/time dial that is used to set the temperature and cooking time can be used to select the bread slices and their brownness when they need to be toasted using the Toast cooking program of the Instant Omni toaster oven.

3. **Bake**

It is used to bake cakes, brownies, or bread in quick time.

4. **Broil**

The broiler's settings provide direct top-down heat to crisp meat, melt cheese, and caramelize vegetables and fruits. It has the default highest temperature, that is 450 degrees F.

5. **Roast**

This cooking program is suitable for roasting meats and vegetables.

6. **Slow Cooker**

The Slow Cook program lets you adjust greater cooking time and lowest temperatures based on the requirements.

7. **Reheat**

Using this mode, the users can warm up leftover food without overcooking the food.

8. **Dehydrate**

Low-temperature heat is regulated to effectively remove moisture from foods, thus giving perfect crispy veggie chips, jerky, and dehydrated fruits.

Meal Preparation and Cooking Method

Cooking all sorts of meals in the Instant Omni Plus is like a breeze. Following are steps to prepare a fresh and good meal in no time:

1. **Prepare the Appliance**

Plugin your appliance, and you will the display lighting up instantly. Make sure the appliance is placed over a flat and stable surface. Place the crumb tray inside the oven at the bottom.

2. **Set the Accessories**

Think about what cooking modes you are going to use and then select the accessories accordingly. Set the steel racks in any of the three portions to set the food. Use Air fryer basket, or the baking pans or tray, or fix the rotisserie stick in the rotisserie catch.

3. **Preheat when Needed**

To preheat the toaster oven, select the required cooking program and temperature. The preset dial on the left side of the screen is used to select the program then adjust the time and temperature using the temp/time dial. Also, select the cooking mode: rotate: to cook food rotisserie or the convection mode to cook other food. The oven will then go into the preheating mode upon pressing the start button; at this point, the timer will not start ticking.

4. **Place the Food Inside**

When the appliance is preheated, the display will indicate that along with a beep. Now you can place the food inside and then close the oven door. If you don't want to preheat the appliance, then you can also set the cooking modes, temperature, and time after placing the food. When its food is all set and ready to cook, then you can hit the start the button, and it will initiate cooking.

5. **Flip and turn the food**

When the food requires to be tossed, turned, or flipped, then the LED display will the word FLIP on the screen. The cooking function is paused when you open the oven door and flip the food. Now you can resume the cooking by pressing the start button. The appliance beeps at the end of the cooking program. It's time to serve the food.

Cleaning and Storage

The instant Omni toaster oven must be cleaned after every cooking session like any other cooking appliance. It is important to keep the inside of the oven germs free all the time. The food particles that are stuck at the base or on the walls of the oven should be cleaned after every session using the following steps:

1. Unplug the Instant Omni toaster oven and allow it to cool down completely. Keep the door open while it cools down.
2. Now remove all the trays, dripping pan, the steel racks, and other accessories from inside the oven.
3. Place the removable parts of the oven in the dishwasher and wash them thoroughly.
4. Once these accessories are washed, all of them dry out completely.
5. Meanwhile, take a clean and slightly damp cloth to clean the inside of the oven.

6. Wipe all the internal walls of the oven using this cloth. Be gentle while you do the wiping.
7. Now use another cloth to clean the exterior of the appliance. Wipe off all the surfaces, especially the touchscreen.
8. Now that everything is clean, you can place the steel racks and dripping pan back to their position for the next session of cooking.
9. For cleaning, do not immerse your appliance in the water directly.
10. To clean the power plug, use a dry piece of cloth to remove the dirt.

Chapter 2: Breakfast Recipes

Simple Bread

Preparation Time: 15 minutes
Cooking Time: 25 minutes
Servings: 10

Ingredients:

- 2 tablespoons unsalted butter, melted
- 1½ teaspoons active dry yeast
- 1½ teaspoons sugar
- 1½ teaspoons kosher salt
- 2 2/3 cups all-purpose flour

Method:

1. In a stand mixer fitted with the dough hook attachment the butter, yeast, sugar, salt and water and mix on low speed, adding ½ cup of the flour at a time.
2. After adding all the flour, mix on medium speed for about 8 minutes.
3. Place the dough into a 6x3-inch round baking pan.
4. With a plastic wrap, cover the bowl and set aside in room temperature for about 1 hour or until doubled in size.
5. Arrange the drip pan in the bottom of Instant Omni Pro Air Fryer Oven Combo.
6. Place the baking pan over the drip pan.
7. Select "Bake" and then adjust the temperature to 400 degrees F.
8. Set the timer for 25 minutes and press "Start".
9. When the display shows "Add Food" place the baking pan over the drip pan.
10. When the display shows "Turn Food" rotate the baking pan.
11. When cooking time is complete, remove the pan from Toaster Oven and place the pan onto a wire rack for about 10-15 minutes.
12. Carefully, invert the bread onto the wire rack to cool completely before slicing.
13. Cut the bread into desired size slices and serve.

Nutritional Information per Serving:

- Calories 146
- Total Fat 2.7 g
- Saturated Fat 1.5 g
- Cholesterol 6 mg
- Sodium 366 mg
- Total Carbs 26.3 g
- Fiber 1 g
- Sugar 0.7 g
- Protein 3.7 g

Tomato Quiche

Preparation Time: 15 minutes
Cooking Time: 30 minutes
Servings: 2

Ingredients:

- 4 eggs
- ¼ cup scallion, chopped
- ½ cup fresh plum tomatoes, chopped
- ½ cup unsweetened almond milk
- 1 cup Cheddar cheese, shredded
- Salt and freshly ground black pepper, as required

Method:

1. In a small baking dish, add all the ingredients and mix well.
2. Arrange the baking dish in the center of Instant Omni Pro Air Fryer Oven Combo.
3. Select "Air Fry" and then adjust the temperature to 340 degrees F.
4. Set the timer for 30 minutes and press "Start".
5. When the display shows "Turn Food" do nothing.
6. When cooking time is complete, remove the baking dish from Toaster Oven.
7. Cut into equal-sized wedges and serve.

Nutritional Information per Serving:

- Calories 378
- Total Fat 28.5 g
- Saturated Fat 14.7 g
- Cholesterol 387 mg
- Sodium 604 mg
- Total Carbs 5.1 g
- Fiber 1.1 g
- Sugar 3.1 g
- Protein 26.2 g

Date Bread

Preparation Time: 15 minutes
Cooking Time: 22 minutes
Servings: 10

Ingredients:

- 2½ cup dates, pitted and chopped
- ¼ cup butter
- 1 cup hot water
- 1½ cups flour
- ½ cup brown sugar
- 1 teaspoon baking powder
- 1 teaspoon baking soda
- ½ teaspoon salt
- 1 egg

Method:

1. In a large bowl, add the dates, butter and top with the hot water.
2. Set aside for about 5 minutes.
3. In a separate bowl, mix together the flour, brown sugar, baking powder, baking soda and salt.
4. In the bowl of dates, add the flour mixture and egg and mix well.
5. Place the mixture into a greased baking pan.
6. Arrange the drip pan in the bottom of Instant Omni Pro Air Fryer Oven Combo.
7. Place the baking pan over the drip pan.
8. Select "Air Fry" and then adjust the temperature to 340 degrees F.
9. Set the timer for 22 minutes and press "Start".
10. When the display shows "Turn Food" do nothing.
11. When cooking time is complete, remove the pan from Toaster Oven and place the pan onto a wire rack for about 10-15 minutes.
12. Carefully, invert the bread onto the wire rack to cool completely before slicing.
13. Cut the bread into desired size slices and serve.

Nutritional Information per Serving:

- Calories 269
- Total Fat 5.4 g
- Saturated Fat 3.1 g
- Cholesterol 29 mg
- Sodium 285 mg
- Total Carbs 55.1 g
- Fiber 64.1 g
- Sugar 35.3 g
- Protein 3.6 g

Bacon, Kale & Tomato Frittata

Preparation Time: 15 minutes
Cooking Time: 16 minutes
Servings: 2

Ingredients:

- ¼ cup bacon, chopped
- ¼ cup fresh kale, tough ribs removed and chopped
- ½ of tomato, cubed
- 3 eggs
- Salt and ground black pepper, as required
- ¼ cup Parmesan cheese, grated

Method:

1. Heat a nonstick skillet over medium heat and cook the bacon for about 5 minutes.
2. Add the kale and cook for about 1-2 minutes.
3. Add the tomato and cook for about 2-3 minutes.
4. Remove from the heat and drain the grease from skillet.
5. Set aside to cool slightly.
6. Meanwhile, in a small bowl, add the eggs, salt and black pepper and beat well.
7. In a greased baking dish, place the bacon mixture and top with the eggs, followed by the cheese.
8. Arrange the baking dish in the center of Instant Omni Pro Air Fryer Oven Combo.
9. Select "Air Fry" and then adjust the temperature to 355 degrees F.
10. Set the timer for 8 minutes and press "Start".
11. When the display shows "Turn Food" do nothing.
12. When cooking time is complete, remove the baking dish from Toaster Oven.
13. Cut into equal-sized wedges and serve.

Nutritional Information per Serving:

- Calories 293
- Total Fat 19.7 g
- Saturated Fat 9.8 g
- Cholesterol 279 mg
- Sodium 935 mg
- Total Carbs 3.4 g

- Fiber 0.3 g
- Sugar 0.9 g
- Protein 25.4 g

Tofu & Mushroom Omelet

Preparation Time: 15 minutes
Cooking Time: 33 minutes
Servings: 2

Ingredients:

- 2 teaspoons canola oil
- ¼ of onion, chopped
- 1 garlic clove, minced
- 8 ounces silken tofu, drained, pressed and sliced
- 3½ ounces fresh mushrooms, sliced
- Salt and freshly ground black pepper, as needed
- 3 eggs, beaten

Method:

1. In a frying pan, heat the oil over medium heat and sauté the onion and garlic for about 3-4 minutes.
2. Add the mushrooms and cook for about 3-4 minutes.
3. Stir in the mushrooms, salt and black pepper and remove from the heat.
4. Transfer the mixture into a baking dish.
5. Arrange the baking dish in the center of Instant Omni Pro Air Fryer Oven Combo.
6. Select "Air Fry" and then adjust the temperature to 355 degrees F.
7. Set the timer for 25 minutes and press "Start".
8. When the display shows "Turn Food" stir the mixture.
9. When cooking time is complete, remove the baking dish from Toaster Oven.
10. Cut the omelet into 2 portions and serve hot

Nutritional Information per Serving:

- Calories 224
- Total Fat 14.5 g
- Saturated Fat 2.9 g
- Cholesterol 246 mg
- Sodium 214 mg
- Total Carbs 6.6 g
- Fiber 0.9 g
- Sugar 3.4 g
- Protein 17.9 g

Cheesy Egg Toasts

Preparation Time: 10 minutes
Cooking Time: 10 minutes
Servings: 2

Ingredients:

- 4 bread slices
- 4 teaspoons unsalted butter
- Salt and ground black pepper, as required
- 4 eggs
- 4 teaspoon cheddar cheese, shredded

Method:

1. With a butter knife, press the crust edges of each bread slice to create the rectangle.
2. With a teaspoon, gently press the bread down to form the inside of the rectangle without tearing.
3. Season each bread slice with salt and black pepper lightly.
4. Carefully, crack one egg into the center of each bread slice.
5. Season the egg with salt and black pepper.
6. Spread the butter over the edges of each slice. (Avoid to touch the butter to eggs).
7. Now sprinkle the cheese onto the butter.
8. Arrange the bread slices onto a greased cooking tray.
9. Arrange the drip pan in the bottom of Instant Omni Pro Air Fryer Oven Combo.
10. Insert the cooking tray in the center position.
11. Select "Bake" and then adjust the temperature to 350 degrees F.
12. Set the timer for 10 minutes and press "Start".
13. When the display shows "Add Food" place the baking pan over the drip pan.
14. When the display shows "Turn Food" do nothing.
15. When cooking time is complete, remove the cooking tray from Toaster Oven and serve immediately.

Nutritional Information per Serving:

- Calories 260
- Total Fat 18.5 g

- Saturated Fat 8.7 g
- Cholesterol 353 mg
- Sodium 407 mg
- Total Carbs 9.9 g
- Fiber 0.4 g
- Sugar 1.5 g
- Protein 13.7 g

Oats & Cranberry Muffins

Preparation Time: 15 minutes
Cooking Time: 10 minutes
Servings: 4

Ingredients:

- ½ cup flour
- ¼ cup rolled oats
- 1/8 teaspoon baking powder
- ½ cup powdered sugar
- ½ cup butter, softened
- 2 eggs
- ¼ teaspoon vanilla extract
- ¼ cup dried cranberries

Method:

1. In a bowl, mix together the flour, oats, and baking powder.
2. In another bowl, add the sugar, and butter. Beat until you get the creamy texture.
3. Then, add in the egg and vanilla extract and beat until well combined.
4. Add the egg mixture into oat mixture and mix until just combined.
5. Fold in the cranberries.
6. Place the mixture into 4 greased muffin molds evenly.
7. Arrange a sheet pan in the center of Instant Omni Pro Air Fryer Oven Combo.
8. Place the muffin molds over the sheet pan.
9. Select "Air Fry" and then adjust the temperature to 355 degrees F.
10. Set the timer for 10 minutes and press "Start".
11. When the display shows "Turn Food" do nothing.
12. When cooking time is complete, remove the muffin molds from Toaster Oven and place the pan onto a wire rack for about 10 minutes.
13. Carefully, invert the muffins onto the wire rack to completely cool before serving.

Nutritional Information per Serving:

- Calories 374
- Total Fat 25.7 g

- Saturated Fat 15.3 g
- Cholesterol 143 mg
- Sodium 195 mg
- Total Carbs 31.3 g
- Fiber 1.2 g
- Sugar 15.3 g
- Protein 5.3 g

Pumpkin Bread

Preparation Time: 15 minutes
Cooking Time: 1 hour
Servings: 8

Ingredients:

- 1 cup all-purpose flour
- ½ teaspoon baking soda
- ¼ teaspoon ground cinnamon
- ¼ teaspoon ground nutmeg
- 1/8 teaspoon ground ginger
- 1/8 teaspoon ground cloves
- 1/8 teaspoon salt
- 1 egg
- 1 cup pumpkin puree
- ¾ cup white sugar
- ¼ cup vegetable oil
- ¼ cup walnuts, chopped

Method:

1. In a bowl, add the flour, baking soda, spices and salt and mix well.
2. In another bowl, add the egg, pumpkin puree, sugar and oil and beat until well combined.
3. Slowly, add the flour mixture and mix until well combined.
4. Lightly, dust a small greased loaf pan with flour and gently tap off the excess.
5. Place the mixture into the prepared loaf pan.
6. With a piece of foil, cover the loaf pan.
7. Arrange the drip pan in the bottom of Instant Omni Pro Air Fryer Oven Combo.
8. Place the loaf pan over the drip pan.
9. Select "Bake" and then adjust the temperature to 350 degrees F.
10. Set the timer for 1 hour and press "Start".
11. When the display shows "Turn Food" rotate the baking pan.

12. When cooking time is complete, remove the pan from Toaster Oven and place the pan onto a wire rack for about 10-15 minutes.
13. Carefully, invert the bread onto the wire rack to cool completely before slicing.
14. Cut the bread into desired size slices and serve.

Nutritional Information per Serving:

- Calories 231
- Total Fat 10 g
- Saturated Fat 1.7 g
- Cholesterol 20 mg
- Sodium 124 mg
- Total Carbs 33.7 g
- Fiber 1.6 g
- Sugar 19.9 g
- Protein 3.6 g

Spinach Muffins

Preparation Time: 15 minutes
Cooking Time: 10 minutes
Servings: 2

Ingredients:

- 2 large eggs
- 2 tablespoons heavy cream
- 2 tablespoons frozen spinach, thawed
- 4 teaspoons ricotta cheese, crumbled
- Salt and ground black pepper, as required

Method:

1. Grease 2 ramekins.
2. In each prepared ramekin, crack 1 egg.
3. Divide the cream spinach, cheese, salt and black pepper in each ramekin and gently stir to combine, without breaking the yolks.
4. Arrange a sheet pan in the center of Instant Omni Pro Air Fryer Oven Combo.
5. Place the muffin molds over the sheet pan.
6. Select "Air Fry" and then adjust the temperature to 330 degrees F.
7. Set the timer for 10 minutes and press "Start".
8. When the display shows "Turn Food" do nothing.
9. When cooking time is complete, remove the muffin molds from Toaster Oven and place the pan onto a wire rack for about 10 minutes.
10. Carefully, invert the muffins onto the platter and serve warm.

Nutritional Information per Serving:

- Calories 138
- Total Fat 11.4 g
- Saturated Fat 5.5 g
- Cholesterol 210 mg
- Sodium 168 mg
- Total Carbs 1.4 g
- Fiber 0 g
- Sugar 0.5 g
- Protein 7.8 g

Chicken Omelet

Preparation Time: 10 minutes
Cooking Time: 10 minutes
Servings: 2

Ingredients:

- 1 teaspoon olive oil
- 2 scallions, chopped
- ½ jalapeño pepper, seeded and chopped
- 3 eggs
- Salt and ground black pepper, as required
- ¼ cup cooked bacon, chopped

Method:

1. In a frying pan, heat the oil over medium heat and cook the scallion for about 2-3 minutes.
2. Add the jalapeño pepper and cook for about 1 minute.
3. Remove from the heat and set aside to cool slightly.
4. Meanwhile, in a bowl, add the eggs, salt, and black pepper and beat well.
5. Add the scallion mixture and chicken and stir to combine.
6. Place the chicken mixture into a small baking dish.
7. Arrange the baking dish in the center of Instant Omni Pro Air Fryer Oven Combo.
8. Select "Air Fry" and then adjust the temperature to 355 degrees F.
9. Set the timer for 6 minutes and press "Start".
10. When the display shows "Turn Food" do nothing.
11. When cooking time is complete, remove the baking dish from Toaster Oven.
12. Cut the omelet into 2 portions and serve hot.

Nutritional Information per Serving:

- Calories 272
- Total Fat 20.6 g
- Saturated Fat 6.2 g
- Cholesterol 276 mg
- Sodium 819 mg
- Total Carbs 2.2 g
- Fiber 0.5 g
- Sugar 1 g
- Protein 19 g

Chapter 3: Vegetarian Recipes

Stuffed Tomatoes

Preparation Time: 15 minutes
Cooking Time: 15 minutes
Servings: 2

Ingredients:

- 2 large tomatoes
- ½ cup broccoli, chopped finely
- ½ cup Cheddar cheese, shredded
- Salt and ground black pepper, as required
- 1 tablespoon unsalted butter, melted
- ½ teaspoon dried thyme, crushed

Method:

1. Carefully, cut the top of each tomato and scoop out pulp and seeds.
2. In a bowl, mix together chopped broccoli, cheese, salt and black pepper.
3. Stuff each tomato with broccoli mixture evenly.
4. Arrange the stuffed tomatoes into the greased air fryer basket.
5. Arrange the fryer basket in the center of Instant Omni Pro Air Fryer Oven Combo.
6. Select "Air Fry" and then adjust the temperature to 355 degrees F.
7. Set the timer for 15 minutes and press "Start".
8. When the display shows "Turn Food" do nothing.
9. When cooking time is complete, remove the tomatoes from Toaster Oven.
10. Serve with the garnishing of thyme.

Nutritional Information per Serving:

- Calories 206
- Total Fat 15.6 g
- Saturated Fat 9.7 g
- Cholesterol 45 mg
- Sodium 310 mg
- Total Carbs 9.1 g
- Fiber 2.9 g
- Sugar 5.3 g

- Protein 9.4 g

Brussels Sprout Salad

Preparation Time: 15 minutes
Cooking Time: 15 minutes
Servings: 4

Ingredients:

For Salad:

- 1 pound fresh medium Brussels sprouts, trimmed and halved vertically
- 3 teaspoons olive oil
- Salt and ground black pepper, as required
- 2 apples, cored and chopped
- 1 red onion, sliced
- 4 cups lettuce, torn

For Dressing:

- 2 tablespoons extra-virgin olive oil
- 2 tablespoons fresh lemon juice
- 1 tablespoon apple cider vinegar
- 1 tablespoon honey
- 1 teaspoon Dijon mustard
- Salt and ground black pepper, as required

Method:

1. For Brussels sprout: in a bowl, add the Brussels sprout, oil, salt, and black pepper and toss to coat well.
2. Spread the Brussels sprouts onto a sheet pan.
3. Arrange the baking sheet in the center of Instant Omni Pro Air Fryer Oven Combo.
4. Select "Air Fry" and then adjust the temperature to 360 degrees F.
5. Set the timer for 15 minutes and press "Start".
6. When the display shows "Turn Food" flip the Brussels sprout.
7. When cooking time is complete, remove the baking sheet from Toaster Oven.

8. Transfer the Brussel sprouts onto a plate and set aside to cool slightly.
9. In a serving bowl, mix together the Brussel sprouts, apples, onion, and lettuce.
10. For dressing: in a bowl, add all the ingredients and beat until well combined.
11. Place the dressing over salad and gently, stir to combine.
12. Serve immediately.

Nutritional Information per Serving:

- Calories 235
- Total Fat 11.3 g
- Saturated Fat 1.7 g
- Cholesterol 0 mg
- Sodium 88 mg
- Total Carbs 34.5 g
- Fiber 8 g
- Sugar 20.3 g
- Protein 4.9 g

Sweet & Spicy Parsnips

Preparation Time: 15 minutes
Cooking Time: 44 minutes
Servings: 5

Ingredients:

- 1½ pounds parsnip, peeled and cut into 1-inch chunks
- 1 tablespoon butter, melted
- 2 tablespoons honey
- 1 tablespoon dried parsley flakes, crushed
- ¼ teaspoon red pepper flakes, crushed
- Salt and ground black pepper, as required

Method:

1. In a large bowl, mix together the parsnips and butter.
2. Arrange the parsnip chunks into the greased air fryer basket in a single layer.
3. Arrange the fryer basket in the center of Instant Omni Pro Air Fryer Oven Combo.
4. Select "Air Fry" and then adjust the temperature to 355 degrees F.
5. Set the timer for 44 minutes and press "Start".
6. Meanwhile, in another large bowl, mix together the remaining ingredients.
7. When the display shows "Turn Food" flip the parsnips chunks.
8. After 40 minutes of cooking, coat the parsnips chunks with honey mixture.
9. When cooking time is complete, remove the air fryer basket from Toaster Oven.
10. Serve hot.

Nutritional Information per Serving:

- Calories 149
- Total Fat 2.7 g
- Saturated Fat 1.5 g
- Cholesterol 6 mg
- Sodium 62 mg
- Total Carbs 31.5 g
- Fiber 6.7 g
- Sugar 13.5 g
- Protein 1.7 g

Jacket Potatoes

Preparation Time: 15 minutes
Cooking Time: 20 minutes
Servings: 2

Ingredients:

- 2 potatoes
- 1 tablespoon mozzarella cheese, shredded
- 3 tablespoons sour cream
- 1 tablespoon butter, softened
- 1 teaspoon chives, minced
- Salt and ground black pepper, as required

Method:

1. With a fork, prick the potatoes.
2. Arrange potatoes into the greased air fryer basket.
3. Arrange the fryer basket in the center of Instant Omni Pro Air Fryer Oven Combo.
4. Select "Air Fry" and then adjust the temperature to 355 degrees F.
5. Set the timer for 20 minutes and press "Start".
6. When the display shows "Turn Food" do nothing.
7. When cooking time is complete, remove from Toaster Oven and transfer the potatoes onto a platter.
8. In a bowl, add the remaining ingredients and mix until well combined.
9. Open potatoes from the center and stuff them with cheese mixture.
10. Serve immediately

Nutritional Information per Serving:

- Calories 227
- Total Fat 12.2 g
- Saturated Fat 7.6 g
- Cholesterol 31mg
- Sodium 226 mg
- Total Carbs 34.8 g
- Fiber 5.1 g
- Sugar 2.5 g
- Protein 8.2 g

Glazed Carrots

Preparation Time: 15 minutes
Cooking Time: 12 minutes
Servings: 4

Ingredients:

- 3 cups carrots, peeled and cut into large chunks
- 1 tablespoon olive oil
- 1 tablespoon maple syrup
- 1 tablespoon fresh parsley, minced
- Salt and ground black pepper, as required

Method:

1. In a bowl, add the carrot, oil, maple syrup, thyme, salt, and black pepper.
2. Arrange the carrot chunks into the greased air fryer basket in a single layer.
3. Arrange the fryer basket in the center of Instant Omni Pro Air Fryer Oven Combo.
4. Select "Air Fry" and then adjust the temperature to 390 degrees F.
5. Set the timer for 12 minutes and press "Start".
6. When the display shows "Turn Food" flip the carrot chunks.
7. When cooking time is complete, remove the air fryer basket from Toaster Oven.
8. Serve hot.

Nutritional Information per Serving:

- Calories 77
- Total Fat 3.5 g
- Saturated Fat 0.5 g
- Cholesterol 0 mg
- Sodium 97 mg
- Total Carbs 11.5 g
- Fiber 2.1 g
- Sugar 7.1 g
- Protein 0.7 g

Parmesan Broccoli

Preparation Time: 10 minutes
Cooking Time: 1520 minutes
Servings: 2

Ingredients:

- 10 ounces frozen broccoli
- 3 tablespoons balsamic vinegar
- 1 tablespoon olive oil
- Salt and ground black pepper, as required
- 2 tablespoons Parmesan cheese, grated
- 1 teaspoon fresh lemon zest, grated

Method:

1. In a bowl, add the broccoli, vinegar, oil, salt, and black pepper and toss to coat well.
2. Arrange the broccoli florets into the greased air fryer basket.
3. Arrange the fryer basket in the center of Instant Omni Pro Air Fryer Oven Combo.
4. Select "Air Fry" and then adjust the temperature to 400 degrees F.
5. Set the timer for 15 minutes and press "Start".
6. When the display shows "Turn Food" flip the broccoli florets.
7. When cooking time is complete, remove the air fryer basket from Toaster Oven.
8. Transfer the broccoli onto serving plates.
9. Immediately, sprinkle with cheese and lemon zest and serve hot.

Nutritional Information per Serving:

- Calories 134
- Total Fat 8.9 g
- Saturated Fat 1.9 g
- Cholesterol 4 mg
- Sodium 210 mg
- Total Carbs 10 g
- Fiber 3.8 g
- Sugar 2.6 g
- Protein 5.9 g

Potato Salad

Preparation Time: 15 minutes
Cooking Time: 40 minutes
Servings: 6

Ingredients:

- 4 russet potatoes
- 1 tablespoon vegetable oil
- Salt, as required
- 3 hard-boiled eggs, peeled and chopped
- 1 cup celery, chopped
- ½ cup red onion, chopped
- 1 tablespoon prepared mustard
- ¼ teaspoon celery salt
- ¼ teaspoon garlic salt
- ¼ cup mayonnaise

Method:

1. With a fork, prick the potatoes.
2. Drizzle the potatoes with oil and rub with the salt.
3. Arrange potatoes into the greased air fryer basket.
4. Arrange the fryer basket in the center of Instant Omni Pro Air Fryer Oven Combo.
5. Select "Air Fry" and then adjust the temperature to 390 degrees F.
6. Set the timer for 40 minutes and press "Start".
7. When the display shows "Turn Food" do nothing.
8. When cooking time is complete, remove the potatoes from Toaster Oven.
9. Transfer the potatoes into a bowl and set aside to cool.
10. After cooling, chop the potatoes.
11. In a serving bowl, add the potatoes and remaining ingredients and gently, mix them well.
12. Refrigerate to chill before serving.

Nutritional Information per Serving:

- Calories 203
- Total Fat 8.5 g
- Saturated Fat 1.7 g
- Cholesterol 84 mg
- Sodium 150 mg
- Total Carbs 27 g
- Fiber 4.2 g
- Sugar 3.2 g
- Protein 6 g

Buttered Zucchini

Preparation Time: 15 minutes
Cooking Time: 30 minutes
Servings: 6

Ingredients:

- 2 tablespoons butter, melted and
- 2 pounds zucchinis, sliced
- 1 tablespoon fresh basil, chopped
- Salt and ground black pepper, as required

Method:

1. In a bowl, mix together all the ingredients.
2. Arrange the zucchini slices into the greased air fryer basket in a single layer.
3. Arrange the fryer basket in the center of Instant Omni Pro Air Fryer Oven Combo.
4. Select "Air Fry" and then adjust the temperature to 400 degrees F.
5. Set the timer for 30 minutes and press "Start".
6. When the display shows "Turn Food" flip the zucchini.
7. When cooking time is complete, remove the air fryer basket from Toaster Oven.
8. Serve hot.

Nutritional Information per Serving:

- Calories 58
- Total Fat 4.1 g
- Saturated Fat 2.5 g
- Cholesterol 10 mg
- Sodium 70 mg
- Total Carbs 5.1 g
- Fiber 1.7 g
- Sugar 2.6 g
- Protein 1.9 g

Tofu in Orange Sauce

Preparation Time: 20 minutes
Cooking Time: 20 minutes
Servings: 4

Ingredients:

For Tofu:

- 1-pound extra-firm tofu, pressed and cubed
- 1 tablespoon cornstarch
- 1 tablespoon low-sodium soy sauce

For Sauce:

- ½ cup water
- 1/3 cup fresh orange juice
- 1 tablespoon maple syrup
- 1 teaspoon orange zest, grated
- 1 teaspoon garlic, minced
- 1 teaspoon fresh ginger, minced
- 2 teaspoons cornstarch
- ¼ teaspoon red pepper flakes, crushed
- 2 scallions, chopped

Method:

1. In a bowl, add the tofu, cornstarch, and soy sauce and toss to coat well.
2. Set the tofu aside to marinate for at least 15 minutes.
3. Arrange the tofu cubes into the greased air fryer basket in a single layer.
4. Arrange the fryer basket in the center of Instant Omni Pro Air Fryer Oven Combo.
5. Select "Air Fry" and then adjust the temperature to 390 degrees F.
6. Set the timer for 10 minutes and press "Start".
7. When the display shows "Turn Food" flip the tofu.
8. Meanwhile, for the sauce: in a small pan, add all the ingredients except for scallions over medium-high heat and bring to a boil, stirring continuously.

9. When cooking time is complete, remove the air fryer basket from Toaster Oven.
10. Transfer the tofu into a serving bowl
11. Top with the sauce and gently stir to combine.
12. Garnish with scallions and serve.

Nutritional Information per Serving:

- Calories 140
- Total Fat 6.7 g
- Saturated Fat 0.6 g
- Cholesterol 0 mg
- Sodium 232 mg
- Total Carbs 11.1 g
- Fiber 0.9 g
- Sugar 5.7 g
- Protein 11.9 g

Chapter 4: Poultry Recipes

Simple Roasted Chicken

Preparation Time: 15 minutes

Cooking Time: 40 minutes

Servings: 3

Ingredients:

- 1 (1½-pounds) whole chicken
- Salt and ground black pepper, as required

Method:

1. Season the chicken with salt and black pepper.
2. Arrange the chicken into the greased air fryer basket, breast-side down.
3. Arrange the fryer basket in the center of Instant Omni Pro Air Fryer Oven Combo.
4. Select "Air Fry" and then adjust the temperature to 390 degrees F.
5. Set the timer for 40 minutes and press "Start".
6. When the display shows "Turn Food" do nothing.
7. When cooking time is complete, remove the air fryer basket from Toaster Oven.
8. Place the chicken onto a platter for about 5-10 minutes before carving.
9. With a sharp knife, cut the chicken into desired sized pieces and serve.

Nutritional Information per Serving:

- Calories 431
- Total Fat 16.8 g
- Saturated Fat 4.6 g
- Cholesterol 202 mg
- Sodium 245 mg
- Total Carbs 0 g
- Fiber 0 g
- Sugar 0 g
- Protein 65.6 g

Crispy Chicken Breast

Preparation Time: 15 minutes
Cooking Time: 40 minutes
Servings: 3

Ingredients:

- ¼ cup all-purpose flour
- 1 large egg, beaten
- ¼ cup fresh parsley, chopped
- 1 cup seasoned breadcrumbs
- 3 (5-ounce) boneless, skinless chicken breasts

Method:

1. In a shallow, dish place the flour.
2. In a second shallows dish, mix together the egg and parsley.
3. In a third shallow dish, place breadcrumbs.
4. Coat the chicken breasts with flour, then dip into eggs and finally coat with breadcrumbs.
5. Place the chicken breasts onto a greased sheet pan.
6. Arrange the drip pan in the bottom of Instant Omni Pro Air Fryer Oven Combo.
7. Place the sheet pan over the drip pan.
8. Select "Roast" and then adjust the temperature to 375 degrees F.
9. Set the timer for 40 minutes and press "Start".
10. When the display shows "Turn Food" do nothing.
11. When cooking time is complete, remove the sheet pan from Toaster Oven.
12. Serve hot.

Nutritional Information per Serving:

- Calories 480
- Total Fat 17 g
- Saturated Fat 34 g
- Cholesterol 188 mg
- Sodium 615 mg
- Total Carbs 31.1 g
- Fiber 1.8 g
- Sugar 0.2 g
- Protein 48.3 g

Rosemary Turkey Breast

Preparation Time: 0 minute
Cooking Time: 1 hour 20 minutes
Servings: 6

Ingredients:

- 1 (2¾-pound) bone-in, skin-on turkey breast half
- 2 tablespoons fresh rosemary, minced
- Salt and ground black pepper, as required

Method:

1. Rub the turkey breast with the rosemary, salt and black pepper evenly.
2. Arrange the turkey breast onto a greased baking pan.
3. Arrange the drip pan in the bottom of Instant Omni Pro Air Fryer Oven Combo.
4. Place the baking pan over the drip pan.
5. Select "Bake" and then adjust the temperature to 450 degrees F.
6. Set the timer for 1 hour 20 minutes and press "Start".
7. When the display shows "Turn Food" flip the turkey wings.
8. When cooking time is complete, remove the air baking pan from Toaster Oven.
9. Place the turkey breast onto a cutting board.
10. With a piece of foil, cover the turkey breast for about 20 minutes before slicing.
11. With a sharp knife, cut the turkey breast into desired size slices and serve.

Nutritional Information per Serving:

- Calories 356
- Total Fat 15 g
- Saturated Fat 3.8 g
- Cholesterol 130 mg
- Sodium 288 mg
- Total Carbs 0.7 g
- Fiber 0.5 g
- Sugar 0 g
- Protein 44.6 g

Spicy Chicken Thighs

Preparation Time: 15 minutes
Cooking Time: 20 minutes
Servings: 4

Ingredients:

- 4 (4-ounces) skinless, boneless chicken thighs
- ½ teaspoon cayenne pepper
- ½ teaspoon paprika
- ½ teaspoon ground cumin
- Salt and ground black pepper, as required
- 2 tablespoons olive oil

Method:

1. In a bowl, mix together the spices, salt and black pepper.
2. Rub the chicken thighs with spice mixture evenly and then, brush with melted butter.
3. Place the chicken thighs into a greased baking pan.
4. Arrange the drip pan in the bottom of Instant Omni Pro Air Fryer Oven Combo.
5. Place the baking pan over the drip pan.
6. Select "Bake" and then adjust the temperature to 450 degrees F.
7. Set the timer for 20 minutes and press "Start".
8. When the display shows "Add Food" place the baking pan over the drip pan.
9. When the display shows "Turn Food" do nothing.
10. When cooking time is complete, remove the pan from Toaster Oven.
11. Serve hot.

Nutritional Information per Serving:

- Calories 204
- Total Fat 11.2 g
- Saturated Fat 2.5 g
- Cholesterol 66 mg
- Sodium 80 mg
- Total Carbs 0.4 g
- Fiber 0.2 g
- Sugar 0.1 g
- Protein 25.4 g

Buttered Turkey Wings

Preparation Time: 10 minutes
Cooking Time: 26 minutes
Servings: 4

Ingredients:

- 2 pounds turkey wings
- Salt and ground black pepper, as required
- 3 tablespoons butter, melted

Method:

1. In a large bowl, add the turkey wings, butter, salt and black pepper and mix well.
2. Arrange the turkey wings into the greased air fryer basket in a single layer.
3. Arrange the fryer basket in the center of Instant Omni Pro Air Fryer Oven Combo.
4. Select "Air Fry" and then adjust the temperature to 380 degrees F.
5. Set the timer for 26 minutes and press "Start".
6. Meanwhile, in another large bowl, mix together the remaining ingredients.
7. When the display shows "Turn Food" flip the turkey wings.
8. When cooking time is complete, remove the air fryer basket from Toaster Oven.
9. Serve hot.

Nutritional Information per Serving:

- Calories 546
- Total Fat 31 g
- Saturated Fat 11.6 g
- Cholesterol 284 mg
- Sodium 266 mg
- Total Carbs 0 g
- Fiber 0 g
- Sugar 0 g
- Protein 62.8 g

Sweet & Spicy Chicken Drumsticks

Preparation Time: 15 minutes
Cooking Time: 20 minutes
Servings: 4

Ingredients:

- 1 garlic clove, crushed
- 1 teaspoon cayenne pepper
- 2 teaspoons brown sugar
- 1 tablespoon Dijon mustard
- Salt and ground black pepper, as required
- 1 tablespoon olive oil
- 4 (6-ounce) chicken drumsticks

Method:

1. In a bowl, mix together all ingredients except chicken drumsticks.
2. Rub the chicken with the oil mix and refrigerate to marinate for about 20-30 minutes.
3. Place the chicken drumsticks onto a greased sheet pan.
4. Arrange the sheet pan in the center of Instant Omni Pro Air Fryer Oven Combo.
5. Select "Air Fry" and then adjust the temperature to 390 degrees F.
6. Set the timer for 10 minutes and press "Start".
7. When the display shows "Turn Food" arrange the chicken, breast-side up.
8. Now, adjust the temperature to 300 degrees F.
9. Set the timer for 10 minutes and press "Start".
10. When the display shows "Turn Food" do nothing.
11. When cooking time is complete, remove the sheet pan from Toaster Oven.
12. Serve hot.

Nutritional Information per Serving:

- Calories 328
- Total Fat 13.5 g
- Saturated Fat 3.1g
- Cholesterol 150 mg
- Sodium 220 mg
- Total Carbs 2.2 g

- Fiber 0.3 g
- Sugar 1.6 g
- Protein 47.1 g

Marinated Chicken Legs

Preparation Time: 15 minutes
Cooking Time: 20 minutes
Servings: 4

Ingredients:

- 4 (8-ounce) chicken legs
- 2 tablespoons balsamic vinegar
- 2 teaspoons garlic, minced
- Salt, as required
- 4 tablespoons plain Greek yogurt
- 1 teaspoon red chili powder
- 1 teaspoon ground cumin
- 1 teaspoon ground coriander
- Ground black pepper, as required

Method:

1. In a bowl, add the chicken legs, vinegar, garlic and salt and mix well.
2. Set aside for about 15 minutes.
3. Meanwhile, in another bowl, mix together the yogurt, spices, salt and black pepper.
4. Add the chicken legs into bowl and coat with the spice mixture generously.
5. Cover the bowl of chicken and refrigerate for at least 10-12 hours.
6. Arrange the chicken legs into the greased air fryer basket.
7. Arrange the fryer basket in the center of Instant Omni Pro Air Fryer Oven Combo.
8. Select "Air Fry" and then adjust the temperature to 445 degrees F.
9. Set the timer for 20 minutes and press "Start".
10. When the display shows "Turn Food" do nothing.
11. When cooking time is complete, remove the air fryer basket from Toaster Oven.
12. Serve hot.

Nutritional Information per Serving:

- Calories 450
- Total Fat 17.2 g
- Saturated Fat 4.8 g
- Cholesterol 203 mg

- Sodium 253 mg
- Total Carbs 2.2 g
- Fiber 0.3 g
- Sugar 1.2 g
- Protein 66.7 g

Crispy Chicken Drumsticks

Preparation Time: 15 minutes
Cooking Time: 25 minutes
Servings: 4

Ingredients:

- 4 chicken drumsticks
- 1 tablespoon adobo seasoning
- Salt, as required
- 1 tablespoon onion powder
- 1 tablespoon garlic powder
- ½ tablespoon paprika
- Ground black pepper, as required
- 2 eggs
- 2 tablespoons milk
- 1 cup all-purpose flour
- ¼ cup cornstarch

Method:

1. Season chicken drumsticks with adobo seasoning and a pinch of salt.
2. Set aside for about 5minutes.
3. In a small bowl, add the spices, salt and black pepper and mix well.
4. In a shallow bowl, add the eggs, milk and 1 teaspoon of spice mixture and beat until well combined.
5. In another shallow bowl, add the flour, cornstarch and remaining spice mixture.
6. Coat the chicken drumsticks with flour mixture and tap off the excess.
7. Now, dip the chicken drumsticks in egg mixture
8. Again, coat the chicken drumsticks with flour mixture.
9. Arrange the chicken drumsticks onto a wire rack lined baking sheet and set aside for about 15 minutes.
10. Now, arrange the chicken drumsticks onto a sheet pan and spray the chicken with cooking spray lightly.

11. Arrange the sheet pan in the center of Instant Omni Pro Air Fryer Oven Combo.
12. Select "Air Fry" and then adjust the temperature to 350 degrees F.
13. Set the timer for 25 minutes and press "Start".
14. When the display shows "Turn Food" do nothing.
15. When cooking time is complete, remove the air fryer basket from Toaster Oven.
16. Serve hot.

Nutritional Information per Serving:

- Calories 483
- Total Fat 12.5 g
- Saturated Fat 34 g
- Cholesterol 232 mg
- Sodium 297 mg
- Total Carbs 35.1 g
- Fiber 1.6 g
- Sugar 1.8 g
- Protein 53.7 g

Chapter 5: Beef & Lamb Recipes

Seasoned Beef Roast

Preparation Time: 10 minutes
Cooking Time: 45 minutes
Servings: 8

Ingredients:

- 2½ pounds beef roast
- 1 tablespoon olive oil
- 2 tablespoons Montreal steak seasoning

Method:

1. With kitchen twines, tie the roast into a compact shape.
2. Brush the roast with oil and then rub with seasoning.
3. Arrange the beef roast onto a greased baking pan.
4. Arrange the baking pan in the center of Instant Omni Pro Air Fryer Oven Combo.
5. Select "Air Fry" and then adjust the temperature to 360 degrees F.
6. Set the timer for 45 minutes and press "Start".
7. When the display shows "Turn Food" do nothing.
8. When cooking time is complete, remove the baking pan from Toaster Oven.
9. Place the steak onto a cutting board for about 10-15 minutes before slicing.
10. With a sharp knife, cut the steak into desired size slices and serve.

Nutritional Information per Serving:

- Calories 283
- Total Fat 10.6 g
- Saturated Fat 3.6 g
- Cholesterol 127 mg
- Sodium 653 mg
- Total Carbs 09 g
- Fiber 0 g
- Sugar 0 g
- Protein 43 g

Glazed Skirt Steak

Preparation Time: 15 minutes
Cooking Time: 10 minutes
Servings: 4

Ingredients:

- 1¼ pounds skirt steak
- ½ cup low-sodium soy sauce
- ¼ cup white wine
- 3-4 tablespoons fresh lemon juice
- 2 tablespoons sesame oil
- 3 tablespoons maple syrup
- 1 tablespoon red pepper flakes, crushed
- 2 garlic cloves, minced

Method:

1. In a large resealable bag, place all the ingredients except for the scallions.
2. Seal the bag and shake to mix well.
3. Refrigerate for up to 2 hours.
4. Remove the steak from bag and set aside at room temperature for 20 minutes before cooking.
5. Place the skirt steak onto a greased baking pan.
6. Arrange the drip pan in the bottom of Instant Omni Pro Air Fryer Oven Combo.
7. Place the baking pan over the drip pan.
8. Select "Bake" and then adjust the temperature to 400 degrees F.
9. Set the timer for 10 minutes and press "Start".
10. When the display shows "Turn Food" do nothing.
11. When cooking time is complete, remove the baking pan from Toaster Oven.
12. Place the steak onto a cutting board for about 10-15 minutes before slicing.
13. With a sharp knife, cut the steak into desired size slices and serve.

Nutritional Information per Serving:

- Calories 421
- Total Fat 21.4 g

- Saturated Fat 6.6 g
- Cholesterol 84 mg
- Sodium 1500 mg
- Total Carbs 14 g
- Fiber 0.4 g
- Sugar 11.5 g
- Protein 40.2 g

Sweet & Soup Lamb Chops

Preparation Time: 15 minutes
Cooking Time: 40 minutes
Servings: 3

Ingredients:

- 3 (8-ounce) lamb shoulder chops
- Salt and ground black pepper, as required
- ¼ cup brown sugar
- 2 tablespoons fresh lemon juice

Method:

1. Season the lamb chops with salt and black pepper generously.
2. In a baking pan, place the chops and sprinkle with sugar, followed by the lime juice.
3. Arrange the drip pan in the bottom of Instant Omni Pro Air Fryer Oven Combo.
4. Place the baking pan over the drip pan.
5. Select "Bake" and then adjust the temperature to 376 degrees F.
6. Set the timer for 40 minutes and press "Start".
7. When the display shows "Turn Food" flip the chops.
8. When cooking time is complete, remove the baking pan from Toaster Oven.
9. Serve hot.

Nutritional Information per Serving:

- Calories 390
- Total Fat 18.1 g
- Saturated Fat 6.1 g
- Cholesterol 151 mg
- Sodium 216 mg
- Total Carbs 12.1 g
- Fiber 0 g
- Sugar 11.9 g
- Protein 44.3 g

Leg of Lamb

Preparation Time: 15 minutes
Cooking Time: 1 hour 40 minutes
Servings: 10

Ingredients:

- ¼ cup olive oil
- 4 garlic cloves, chopped
- ¼ cup fresh rosemary
- 3 tablespoons Dijon mustard
- 2 tablespoons maple syrup
- Salt and ground black pepper, as required
- 1 (4-pound) leg of lamb

Method:

1. In a food processor, add the oil, garlic, herbs, mustard, honey, salt and black pepper and pulse until smooth.
2. Place the leg of lamb and marinade into a glass baking dish and mix well
3. With plastic wrap, cover the baking dish and refrigerate to marinate for 6-8 hours.
4. Arrange a wire rack in a baking pan.
5. Arrange the leg of lamb into the prepared baking pan.
6. Arrange the drip pan in the bottom of Instant Omni Pro Air Fryer Oven Combo.
7. Place the baking pan over the drip pan.
8. Select "Bake" and then adjust the temperature to 420 degrees F.
9. Set the timer for 20 minutes and press "Start".
10. After 20 minutes, set the temperature to 320 degrees F for 1 hour and 20 minutes.
11. When cooking time is complete, remove the baking pan from Toaster Oven.
12. Place the leg of lamb onto a cutting board.
13. With a piece of foil, cover the leg of lamb for about 10 minutes before slicing.
14. With a sharp knife, cut the leg of lamb into desired size slices and serve.

Nutritional Information per Serving:

- Calories 401
- Total Fat 18.8 g

- Saturated Fat 5.6 g
- Cholesterol 163 mg
- Sodium 208 mg
- Total Carbs 4.3 g
- Fiber 0.8 g
- Sugar 2.4 g
- Protein 51.3 g

Bacon Wrapped Filet Mignon

Preparation Time: 10 minutes
Cooking Time: 15 minutes
Servings: 2

Ingredients:

- 2 bacon slices
- 2 (6-ounces) filet mignon
- Salt and ground black pepper, as required
- 1 teaspoon olive oil

Method:

1. Wrap 1 bacon slice around each mignon filet and secure with a toothpick.
2. Season the filets with salt and black pepper and then, coat each filet with oil.
3. Place the filets onto a greased air fryer basket.
4. Arrange the air fryer basket in the center of Instant Omni Pro Air Fryer Oven Combo.
5. Select "Air Fry" and then adjust the temperature to 375 degrees F.
6. Set the timer for 15 minutes and press "Start".
7. When the display shows "Turn Food" flip the filets.
8. When cooking time is complete, remove the air fryer basket from Toaster Oven.
9. Serve hot.

Nutritional Information per Serving:

- Calories 348
- Total Fat 15.6 g
- Saturated Fat 5.3 g
- Cholesterol 117 mg
- Sodium 253 mg
- Total Carbs 0 g
- Fiber 0 g
- Sugar 0 g
- Protein 49.2 g

Seasoned Flank Steak

Preparation Time: 10 minutes
Cooking Time: 30 minutes
Servings: 6

Ingredients:

- 2 pounds flank steak
- 3 tablespoons taco seasoning rub

Method:

1. Rub the steak with taco seasoning evenly.
2. Place the steak onto a greased baking pan.
3. Arrange the drip pan in the bottom of Instant Omni Pro Air Fryer Oven Combo.
4. Place the baking pan over the drip pan.
5. Select "Bake" and then adjust the temperature to 425 degrees F.
6. Set the timer for 30 minutes and press "Start".
7. When the display shows "Turn Food" do nothing.
8. When cooking time is complete, remove the baking pan from Toaster Oven.
9. Place the steak onto a cutting board for about 10-15 minutes before slicing.
10. With a sharp knife, cut the steak into desired size slices and serve.

Nutritional Information per Serving:

- Calories 308
- Total Fat 12.6 g
- Saturated Fat 5.2 g
- Cholesterol 83 mg
- Sodium 400 mg
- Total Carbs 3 g
- Fiber 0 g
- Sugar 0.8 g
- Protein 42.1 g

Lemony Flank Steak

Preparation Time: 15 minutes
Cooking Time: 12 minutes
Servings: 6

Ingredients:

- 2 pounds flank steak
- 3 tablespoons fresh lemon juice
- 2 tablespoons olive oil
- 3 garlic cloves, minced
- 1 teaspoon red chili powder
- Salt and ground black pepper, as required

Method:

1. In a large bowl, add all the ingredients except for steak and mix well.
2. Add the flank steak and coat with the marinade generously.
3. Refrigerate to marinate for 24 hours, flipping occasionally.
4. Arrange the steak onto a greased sheet pan.
5. Arrange the baking pan in the top portion of Instant Omni Pro Air Fryer Oven Combo.
6. Select "Broil" and set the timer for 12 minutes and press "Start".
7. When the display shows "Turn Food" flip the steak.
8. When cooking time is complete, remove the air baking pan from Toaster Oven.
9. Place the roast onto a cutting board for about 10-15 minutes before slicing.
10. With a sharp knife, cut the roast into desired size slices and serve.

Nutritional Information per Serving:

- Calories 339
- Total Fat 17.4 g
- Saturated Fat 6 g
- Cholesterol 83 mg
- Sodium 118 mg
- Total Carbs 0.9 g
- Fiber 0.2 g
- Sugar 0.2 g
- Protein 42.3 g

Simple Filet Mignon

Preparation Time: 10 minutes
Cooking Time: 14 minutes
Servings: 2

Ingredients:

- 2 (6-ounces) filet mignon
- 1 tablespoon olive oil
- Salt and ground black pepper, as required

Method:

1. Coat both sides of filet with oil and then, season with salt and black pepper.
2. Place the filets onto a greased air fryer basket.
3. Arrange the air fryer basket in the center of Instant Omni Pro Air Fryer Oven Combo.
4. Select "Air Fry" and then adjust the temperature to 390 degrees F.
5. Set the timer for 14 minutes and press "Start".
6. When the display shows "Turn Food" flip the filets.
7. When cooking time is complete, remove the air fryer basket from Toaster Oven.
8. Serve hot.

Nutritional Information per Serving:

- Calories 364
- Total Fat 18.2 g
- Saturated Fat 5.3 g
- Cholesterol 112 mg
- Sodium 178 mg
- Total Carbs 0 g
- Fiber 0 g
- Sugar 0 g
- Protein 47.8 g

Rosemary Lamb Chops

Preparation Time: 15 minutes
Cooking Time: 6 minutes
Servings: 2

Ingredients:

- 1 tablespoon olive oil, divided
- 2 garlic cloves, minced
- 1 tablespoon fresh rosemary, chopped
- Salt and ground black pepper, as required
- 4 (4-ounce) lamb chops

Method:

1. In a large bowl, mix together the oil, garlic, rosemary, salt and black pepper.
2. Coat the chops with half of the garlic mixture.
3. Place the rack of lamb into a greased air fryer basket.
4. Arrange the air fryer basket in the center of Instant Omni Pro Air Fryer Oven Combo.
5. Select "Air Fry" and then adjust the temperature to 390 degrees F.
6. Set the timer for 6 minutes and press "Start".
7. When the display shows "Turn Food" "do nothing.
8. When cooking time is complete, remove the air fryer basket from Toaster Oven.
9. Serve hot with the topping of remaining garlic mixture.

Nutritional Information per Serving:

- Calories 492
- Total Fat 23.9 g
- Saturated Fat 7.1 g
- Cholesterol 204 mg
- Sodium 251 mg
- Total Carbs 2.1 g
- Fiber 0.8 g
- Sugar 0 g
- Protein 64 g

Crusted Rack of Lamb

Preparation Time: 15 minutes
Cooking Time: 35 minutes
Servings: 6

Ingredients:

- 1¾ pounds rack of lamb
- Salt and ground black pepper, as required
- 1 egg
- 1 tablespoon seasoned breadcrumbs
- 3 ounces pistachios, chopped finely

Method:

1. Season the rack of lamb with salt and black pepper evenly and then, drizzle with cooking spray.
2. In a shallow dish, beat the egg.
3. In another shallow dish mix together breadcrumbs and pistachios.
4. Dip the rack of lamb in egg and then coat with the pistachio mixture.
5. Place the rack of lamb into a greased air fryer basket.
6. Arrange the air fryer basket in the center of Instant Omni Pro Air Fryer Oven Combo.
7. Select "Air Fry" and then adjust the temperature to 220 degrees F.
8. Set the timer for 35 minutes and press "Start".
9. When the display shows "Turn Food" do nothing.
10. After 30 minutes of cooking, adjust the temperature to 390 degrees F.
11. When cooking time is complete, remove the air fryer basket from Toaster Oven.
12. Place the rack onto a cutting board for about 5 minutes.
13. Cut the rack into individual chops and serve hot.

Nutritional Information per Serving:

- Calories 313
- Total Fat 19.2 g
- Saturated Fat 5 g
- Cholesterol 115 mg
- Sodium 221 mg
- Total Carbs 4.6 g
- Fiber 1.5 g
- Sugar 1 g
- Protein 3.8 g

Chapter 6: Pork Recipes

Glazed Pork Ribs

Preparation Time: 10 minutes
Cooking Time: 13 minutes
Servings: 6

Ingredients:

- ¾ cup tomato sauce
- 3 tablespoons honey
- 1 tablespoon Worcestershire sauce
- 1 tablespoon low-sodium soy sauce
- 1 tablespoon fresh lime juice
- ½ teaspoon garlic powder
- ½ teaspoon red pepper flakes, crushed
- Freshly ground black pepper, as required
- 2 pounds pork ribs

Method:

1. In a large bowl, add all the ingredients except pork ribs and mix well.
2. Add the pork ribs ad coat with the mixture generously.
3. Place the pork ribs into a greased air fryer basket.
4. Arrange the air fryer basket in the center of Instant Omni Pro Air Fryer Oven Combo.
5. Select "Air Fry" and then adjust the temperature to 355 degrees F.
6. Set the timer for 13 minutes and press "Start".
7. When the display shows "Turn Food" "flip the chops.
8. When cooking time is complete, remove the air fryer basket from Toaster Oven.
9. Serve hot.

Nutritional Information per Serving:

- Calories 457
- Total Fat 26.9 g
- Saturated Fat 9.5 g
- Cholesterol 15690 mg
- Sodium 423 mg
- Total Carbs 11.3 g

- Fiber 0.6 g
- Sugar 10.7 g
- Protein 40.7 g

Mustard Pork Chops

Preparation Time: 15 minutes
Cooking Time: 12 minutes
Servings: 4

Ingredients:

- 2 garlic cloves, minced
- 1 tablespoon fresh rosemary, chopped
- 2 tablespoons olive oil
- ¾ tablespoon Dijon mustard
- ½ teaspoon ground coriander
- ½ teaspoon ground cumin
- 1 teaspoon sugar
- Salt, as required
- 2 (6-ounces) (1-inch thick) pork chops

Method:

1. In a bowl, mix together the garlic, rosemary, oil, mustard, spices, sugar, and salt.
2. Add the pork chops and coat with marinade evenly.
3. Cover and refrigerate for about 2-3 hours.
4. Remove the chops from the refrigerator and set aside at room temperature for about 30 minutes.
5. Place the pork chops into a greased air fryer basket.
6. Arrange the air fryer basket in the center of Instant Omni Pro Air Fryer Oven Combo.
7. Select "Air Fry" and then adjust the temperature to 390 degrees F.
8. Set the timer for 12 minutes and press "Start".
9. When the display shows "Turn Food" "do nothing.
10. When cooking time is complete, remove the air fryer basket from Toaster Oven.
11. Serve hot.

Nutritional Information per Serving:

- Calories 344
- Total Fat 28.5 g

- Saturated Fat 9 g
- Cholesterol 73 mg
- Sodium 133 mg
- Total Carbs 2.3 g
- Fiber 0.5 g
- Sugar 1.1 g
- Protein 19.4 g

Herbed Pork Loin

Preparation Time: 10 minutes
Cooking Time: 20 minutes
Servings: 6

Ingredients:

- 3 tablespoons sugar
- 1 teaspoon dried basil
- 1 teaspoon dried thyme
- 1 teaspoon dried rosemary
- 1 teaspoon garlic powder
- Salt and ground black pepper, as required
- 2 pounds pork loin

Method:

1. In a bowl, add the sugar, herbs, garlic powder, salt and black pepper and mix well.
2. Rub the pork loin with bail mixture generously.
3. Place the pork loin into a greased air fryer basket.
4. Arrange the air fryer basket in the center of Instant Omni Pro Air Fryer Oven Combo.
5. Select "Air Fry" and then adjust the temperature to 400 degrees F.
6. Set the timer for 20 minutes and press "Start".
7. When the display shows "Turn Food" "do nothing.
8. When cooking time is complete, remove the air fryer basket from Toaster Oven.
9. Place the pork loin onto a cutting board for about 10 minutes before slicing.
10. With a sharp knife, cut the loin into desired sized slices and serve.

Nutritional Information per Serving:

- Calories 391
- Total Fat 21.1 g
- Saturated Fat 7.9 g
- Cholesterol 121 mg
- Sodium 130 mg
- Total Carbs 6.6 g
- Fiber 0.2 g
- Sugar 6.1 g
- Protein 41.4 g

Simple Pork Loin

Preparation Time: 10 minutes
Cooking Time: 30 minutes
Servings: 6

Ingredients:

- 2 pounds pork loin
- 2 tablespoons olive oil, divided
- Salt and ground black pepper, as required

Method:

1. Arrange a wire rack in a baking pan.
2. Coat the pork loin with oil and then, rub with salt and black pepper.
3. Arrange the pork loin into the prepared baking pan.
4. Arrange the drip pan in the bottom of Instant Omni Pro Air Fryer Oven Combo.
5. Place the baking pan over the drip pan.
6. Select "Bake" and then adjust the temperature to 350 degrees F.
7. Set the timer for 30 minutes and press "Start".
8. When cooking time is complete, remove the baking pan from Toaster Oven.
9. Place the pork loin onto a cutting board.
10. With a piece of foil, cover the pork loin for about 10 minutes before slicing.
11. With a sharp knife, cut the pork loin into desired size slices and serve.

Nutritional Information per Serving:

- Calories 406
- Total Fat 25.7 g
- Saturated Fat 8.6 g
- Cholesterol 121 mg
- Sodium 121 mg
- Total Carbs 0 g
- Fiber 0 g
- Sugar 0 g
- Protein 41.3 g

Seasoned Pork Shoulder

Preparation Time: 15 minutes
Cooking Time: 1 hour
Servings: 10

Ingredients:

- 3 pounds skin-on, bone-in pork shoulder
- 2-3 tablespoons adobo seasoning
- Salt, as required

Method:

1. Arrange the pork shoulder onto a cutting board, skin-side down.
2. Season the inner side of pork shoulder with adobo seasoning and salt.
3. Season the inner side of pork shoulder with salt and adobo seasoning
4. With kitchen twines, tie the pork shoulder into a long round cylinder shape.
5. Season the outer side of pork shoulder with salt.
6. Insert the rotisserie rod through the pork shoulder.
7. Insert the rotisserie forks, one on each side of the rod to secure the pork shoulder.
8. Arrange the drip pan in the bottom of Instant Omni Pro Air Fryer Oven Combo.
9. Now, slide the rod's left side into the groove along the metal bar so it doesn't move.
10. Then, close the door and touch "Rotate".
11. Select "Roast" and then adjust the temperature to 350 degrees F.
12. Set the timer for 60 minutes and press the "Start".
13. When cooking time is complete, press the red lever to release the rod.
14. Remove the pork from toaster oven and place onto a platter for about 10 minutes before slicing.
15. With a sharp knife, cut the pork shoulder into desired sized slices and serve.

Nutritional Information per Serving:

- Calories 397
- Total Fat 29.1 g
- Saturated Fat 10.7 g
- Cholesterol 122 mg
- Sodium 176 mg
- Total Carbs 0 g
- Fiber 0 g
- Sugar 0 g

- Protein 31.7 g

Bacon Wrapped Pork Tenderloin

Preparation Time: 15 minutes
Cooking Time: 30 minutes
Servings: 4

Ingredients:

- 1 (1½ pound) pork tenderloin
- 2 tablespoons Dijon mustard
- 1 tablespoon honey
- 4 bacon strips

Method:

1. Coat the tenderloin with mustard and honey.
2. Wrap the pork tenderloin with bacon strips.
3. Place the pork loin into a greased air fryer basket.
4. Arrange the air fryer basket in the center of Instant Omni Pro Air Fryer Oven Combo.
5. Select "Air Fry" and then adjust the temperature to 360 degrees F.
6. Set the timer for 30 minutes and press "Start".
7. When the display shows "Turn Food" "flip the pork tenderloin.
8. When cooking time is complete, remove the air fryer basket from Toaster Oven.
9. Place the pork loin onto a cutting board for about 10 minutes before slicing.
10. With a sharp knife, cut the tenderloin into desired sized slices and serve.

Nutritional Information per Serving:

- Calories 386
- Total Fat 16.1 g
- Saturated Fat 5.7 g
- Cholesterol 164 mg
- Sodium 273 mg
- Total Carbs 4.8 g
- Fiber 0.3 g
- Sugar 4.4 g
- Protein 52.6 g

Glazed Pork Tenderloin

Preparation Time: 15 minutes
Cooking Time: 20 minutes
Servings: 3

Ingredients:

- 2 tablespoons red hot sauce
- 2 tablespoons honey
- 1 tablespoon fresh rosemary, minced
- ¼ teaspoon red pepper flakes, crushed
- Salt, as required
- 1-pound pork tenderloin

Method:

1. In a small bowl, add the hot sauce, honey, rosemary, red pepper flakes and salt and mix well.
2. Brush the pork tenderloin with mixture evenly.
3. Place the pork tenderloin into a greased air fryer basket.
4. Arrange the air fryer basket in the center of Instant Omni Pro Air Fryer Oven Combo.
5. Select "Air Fry" and then adjust the temperature to 350 degrees F.
6. Set the timer for 20 minutes and press "Start".
7. When the display shows "Turn Food" "do nothing.
8. When cooking time is complete, remove the air fryer basket from Toaster Oven.
9. Place the pork tenderloin onto a cutting board for about 10 minutes before slicing.
10. With a sharp knife, cut the tenderloin into desired sized slices and serve.

Nutritional Information per Serving:

- Calories 264
- Total Fat 5.6 g
- Saturated Fat 1.9 g
- Cholesterol 110 mg
- Sodium 391 mg
- Total Carbs 12.5 g
- Fiber 0.6 g
- Sugar 11.6 g
- Protein 39.7 g

Glazed Pork Shoulder

Preparation Time: 15 minutes
Cooking Time: 18 minutes
Servings: 5

Ingredients:

- 1/3 cup soy sauce
- 2 tablespoons brown sugar
- 1 tablespoon maple syrup
- 2 pounds pork shoulder, cut into 1½-inch thick slices

Method:

1. In a large bowl, mix together the soy sauce, brown sugar, and maple syrup.
2. Add the pork shoulder and coat with marinade generously.
3. Cover and refrigerate to marinate for about 4-6 hours.
4. Place the pork shoulder into a greased air fryer basket.
5. Arrange the air fryer basket in the center of Instant Omni Pro Air Fryer Oven Combo.
6. Select “Air Fry” and then adjust the temperature to 355 degrees F.
7. Set the timer for 10 minutes and press “Start”.
8. When the display shows “Turn Food” “do nothing.
9. After 10 minutes adjust the temperature to 390 degrees F for 8 minutes.
10. When cooking time is complete, remove the air fryer basket from Toaster Oven.
11. Place the pork shoulder onto a cutting board for about 10 minutes before slicing.
12. With a sharp knife, cut the tenderloin into desired sized slices and serve.

Nutritional Information per Serving:

- Calories 563
- Total Fat 38.8 g
- Saturated Fat 14.3 g
- Cholesterol 163 mg
- Sodium 1000 mg
- Total Carbs 7.5 g
- Fiber 0.1 g
- Sugar 6.2 g
- Protein 43.3 g

Breaded Pork Chops

Preparation Time: 15 minutes
Cooking Time: 15 minutes
Servings: 3

Ingredients:

- 3 (6-ounce) pork chops
- Salt and ground black pepper, as required
- ¼ cup plain flour
- 1 egg
- 4 ounces seasoned breadcrumbs
- 1 tablespoon canola oil

Method:

1. Season each pork chop with salt and black pepper.
2. In a shallow bowl, place the flour
3. In a second bowl, crack the egg and beat well.
4. In a third bowl, add the breadcrumbs and oil and mix until a crumbly mixture form.
5. Coat the pork chop with flour, then dip into beaten egg and finally, coat with the breadcrumbs mixture.
6. Place the pork chops into a greased air fryer basket.
7. Arrange the air fryer basket in the center of Instant Omni Pro Air Fryer Oven Combo.
8. Select "Air Fry" and then adjust the temperature to 400 degrees F.
9. Set the timer for 15 minutes and press "Start".
10. When the display shows "Turn Food" "flip the chops.
11. When cooking time is complete, remove the air fryer basket from Toaster Oven.
12. Serve hot.

Nutritional Information per Serving:

- Calories 413
- Total Fat 20.2 g
- Saturated Fat 4.4 g
- Cholesterol 119 mg

- Sodium 832 mg
- Total Carbs 31 g
- Fiber 1.6 g
- Sugar 0.1 g
- Protein 28.3 g

Stuffed Pork Roll

Preparation Time: 15 minutes
Cooking Time: 15 minutes
Servings: 4

Ingredients:

- 1 scallion, chopped
- ¼ cup sun-dried tomatoes, chopped finely
- 2 tablespoons fresh parsley, chopped
- Salt and ground black pepper, as required
- 4 (6-ounce) pork cutlets, pounded slightly
- 2 teaspoons paprika
- ½ tablespoon olive oil

Method:

1. In a bowl, mix together, scallion, tomatoes, parsley, salt and black pepper.
2. Coat each cutlet with tomato mixture.
3. Roll each cutlet and secure with cocktail sticks.
4. Rub the outer part of rolls with paprika, salt and black pepper.
5. Coat the rolls with oil evenly.
6. Place the pork rolls into a greased air fryer basket.
7. Arrange the air fryer basket in the center of Instant Omni Pro Air Fryer Oven Combo.
8. Select "Air Fry" and then adjust the temperature to 390 degrees F.
9. Set the timer for 15 minutes and press "Start".
10. When the display shows "Turn Food" "flip the chops.
11. When cooking time is complete, remove the air fryer basket from Toaster Oven.
12. Serve hot.

Nutritional Information per Serving:

- Calories 447
- Total Fat 21 g
- Saturated Fat 2.7 g
- Cholesterol 15 mg
- Sodium 798 mg
- Total Carbs 20.3 g
- Fiber 2.6 g
- Sugar 1.7 g
- Protein 43.9 g

Chapter 7: Snack Recipes

Pancetta Wrapped Shrimp

Preparation Time: 15 minutes
Cooking Time: 7 minutes
Servings: 6

Ingredients:

- 1-pound pancetta, thinly sliced
- 1-pound shrimp, peeled and deveined

Method:

1. Wrap each shrimp with one pancetta slice.
2. Arrange the shrimp in a baking dish and refrigerate for about 20 minutes.
3. Now, place the shrimp into the greased air fryer basket.
4. Arrange the air fryer basket in the center of Instant Omni Pro Air Fryer Oven Combo.
5. Select "Air Fry" and then adjust the temperature to 390 degrees F.
6. Set the timer for 7 minutes and press "Start".
7. When the display shows "Turn Food" do nothing.
8. When cooking time is complete, remove the air fryer basket from Toaster Oven.
9. Serve warm.

Nutritional Information per Serving:

- Calories 499
- Total Fat 32.9 g
- Saturated Fat 10.8 g
- Cholesterol 242 mg
- Sodium 1800 mg
- Total Carbs 2.2 g
- Fiber 0 g
- Sugar 0 g
- Protein 45.2 g

Mozzarella Sticks

Preparation Time: 15 minutes
Cooking Time: 12 minutes
Servings: 3

Ingredients:

- 3 tablespoons all-purpose flour
- 2 eggs
- 3 tablespoons milk
- ½ cup breadcrumbs
- ½ pound mozzarella cheese block, cut into 3x½-inch sticks

Method:

1. In a shallow dish, place the flour.
2. In a second shallow dish, add the eggs and milk and beat well.
3. In a third shallow dish, place the breadcrumbs.
4. Coat the Mozzarella sticks with flour, then dip in egg mixture and finally, coat with the breadcrumbs.
5. Arrange the Mozzarella sticks onto a cookie sheet and freeze for about 1-2 hours.
6. Now, place the mozzarella sticks into the greased air fryer basket.
7. Arrange the air fryer basket in the center of Instant Omni Pro Air Fryer Oven Combo.
8. Select "Air Fry" and then adjust the temperature to 400 degrees F.
9. Set the timer for 12 minutes and press "Start".
10. When the display shows "Turn Food" do nothing.
11. When cooking time is complete, remove the air fryer basket from Toaster Oven.
12. Serve warm.

Nutritional Information per Serving:

- Calories 162
- Total Fat 5.1 g
- Saturated Fat 1.8 g
- Cholesterol 113 mg
- Sodium 209 mg
- Total Carbs 20.1 g
- Fiber 1 g
- Sugar 2.1 g
- Protein 8.7 g

Haddock Nuggets

Preparation Time: 15 minutes
Cooking Time: 8 minutes
Servings: 5

Ingredients:

- 1 cup all-purpose flour
- 2 eggs
- ¾ cup seasoned breadcrumbs
- 2 tablespoons vegetable oil
- 1-pound boneless haddock fillet, cut into strips

Method:

1. In a shallow dish, place the flour.
2. In a second dish, crack the eggs and beat well.
3. In a third dish, mix together the breadcrumbs and oil.
4. Coat the nuggets with flour, then dip into beaten eggs and finally, coat with the breadcrumbs.
5. Place the nuggets into the greased air fryer basket in a single layer.
6. Arrange the air fryer basket in the center of Instant Omni Pro Air Fryer Oven Combo.
7. Select "Air Fry" and then adjust the temperature to 390 degrees F.
8. Set the timer for 8 minutes and press "Start".
9. When the display shows "Turn Food" flip the wings.
10. When cooking time is complete, remove the air fryer basket from Toaster Oven.
11. Serve warm.

Nutritional Information per Serving:

- Calories 311
- Total Fat 10.4 g
- Saturated Fat 1.7 g
- Cholesterol 110 mg
- Sodium 312 mg
- Total Carbs 29.4 g
- Fiber 1.3 g
- Sugar 0.2 g
- Protein 23.6 g

Spinach Chips

Preparation Time: 10 minutes
Cooking Time: 10 minutes
Servings: 2

Ingredients:

- 2 cups fresh baby spinach leaves
- 1 tablespoon canola oil
- Salt and ground black pepper, as required

Method:

1. In a bowl, add all the ingredients and toss to coat well.
2. Place the spinach leaves into the greased air fryer basket in a single layer.
3. Arrange the air fryer basket in the center of Instant Omni Pro Air Fryer Oven Combo/
4. Select "Air Fry" and then adjust the temperature to 300 degrees F.
5. Set the timer for 10 minutes and press "Start".
6. When the display shows "Turn Food" do nothing.
7. When cooking time is complete, remove the air fryer basket from Toaster Oven.
8. Serve warm.

Nutritional Information per Serving:

- Calories 69
- Total Fat 7.1 g
- Saturated Fat 0.5 g
- Cholesterol 0 mg
- Sodium 101 mg
- Total Carbs 1.1 g
- Fiber 0.7 g
- Sugar 0.1 g
- Protein 0.9 g

Spicy Chicken Wings

Preparation Time: 15 minutes
Cooking Time: 20 minutes
Servings: 4

Ingredients:

- 1½ pounds chicken wing sections
- 1 tablespoon canola oil
- Salt and ground black pepper, as required
- ¼ cup hot wing sauce

Method:

1. In a bowl, add the chicken wings, oil, salt and black pepper and mix well.
2. Place the chicken wings into the greased air fryer basket in a single layer.
3. Arrange the air fryer basket in the center of Instant Omni Pro Air Fryer Oven Combo.
4. Select "Air Fry" and then adjust the temperature to 400 degrees F.
5. Set the timer for 20 minutes and press "Start".
6. When the display shows "Turn Food" flip the wings.
7. When cooking time is complete, remove the air fryer basket from Toaster Oven.
8. Coat the chicken wings with wing sauce evenly.
9. Now, arrange the air fryer basket in the top of Instant Omni Pro Air Fryer Oven Combo.
10. Select "Broil" and then set the timer for 1 minute.
11. Press "Start".
12. When cooking time is complete, remove the air fryer basket from Toaster Oven.
13. Serve warm.

Nutritional Information per Serving:

- Calories 354
- Total Fat 16.1 g
- Saturated Fat 3.7 g
- Cholesterol 151 mg
- Sodium 214 mg
- Total Carbs 0 g
- Fiber 0 g
- Sugar 0 g

- Protein 49.2 g

Avocado Fries

Preparation Time: 15 minutes
Cooking Time: 7 minutes
Servings: 4

Ingredients:

- ¼ cup all-purpose flour
- Salt and ground black pepper, as required
- 1 egg
- 1 teaspoon water
- ½ cup seasoned breadcrumbs
- 1 avocado, peeled, pitted and sliced into 8 pieces
- Nonstick cooking spray

Method:

1. In a shallow bowl, mix together the flour, salt, and black pepper.
2. In a second bowl, add the egg and water and beat well.
3. In a third bowl, place the breadcrumbs.
4. Coat the avocado slices with flour mixture, then dip into egg mixture and finally, coat evenly with the breadcrumbs.
5. Now, spray the avocado slices with cooking spray evenly.
6. Place the avocado slices into the greased air fryer basket.
7. Arrange the air fryer basket in the center of Instant Omni Pro Air Fryer Oven Combo.
8. Select "Air Fry" and then adjust the temperature to 400 degrees F.
9. Set the timer for 7 minutes and press "Start".
10. When the display shows "Turn Food" do nothing.
11. When cooking time is complete, remove the air fryer basket from Toaster Oven.
12. Serve warm.

Nutritional Information per Serving:

- Calories 202
- Total Fat 12.7 g
- Saturated Fat 2.4 g
- Cholesterol 41 mg

- Sodium 232 mg
- Total Carbs 18.9 g
- Fiber 4.1 g
- Sugar 0.4 g
- Protein 4.6 g

Chapter 8: Dessert Recipes

Cherry Crumble

Preparation Time: 15 minutes
Cooking Time: 25 minutes
Servings: 4

Ingredients:

- 1 (14-ounce) can cherry pie filling
- ¼ cup butter, softened
- 9 tablespoons self-rising flour
- 7 tablespoons powdered sugar
- Pinch of salt

Method:

1. Lightly, grease a baking dish.
2. Place the cherry pie filling into the prepared baking dish evenly.
3. In a bowl, add the remaining ingredients and mix until a crumbly mixture forms.
4. Spread the mixture over pie filling evenly.
5. Arrange a wire rack in the center of Instant Omni Pro Air Fryer Oven Combo.
6. Place the baking dish onto the wire rack.
7. Select "Air Fry" and then adjust the temperature to 320 degrees F.
8. Set the timer for 25 minutes and press "Start".
9. When the display shows "Turn Food" do nothing.
10. When cooking time is complete, remove the muffin molds from Toaster Oven
11. Place the ramekins onto a wire rack to cool.
12. Refrigerate overnight before serving.
13. Place the baking dish onto a wire rack to cool for about 10 minutes.
14. Serve warm.

Nutritional Information per Serving:

- Calories 334
- Total Fat 11.8 g
- Saturated Fat 7.3 g
- Cholesterol 31 mg
- Sodium 139 mg
- Total Carbs 55.2 g
- Fiber 1.1 g
- Sugar 13.8 g

- Protein 2.3 g

Banana Muffins

Preparation Time: 15 minutes
Cooking Time: 25 minutes
Servings: 12

Ingredients:

- 1 2/3 cups all-purpose flour
- 1 teaspoon baking soda
- 1 teaspoon baking powder
- ½ teaspoon ground cinnamon
- ¼ teaspoon ground nutmeg
- ¼ teaspoon ground ginger
- ½ teaspoon salt
- 4 ripe bananas, peeled and mashed
- 2 eggs
- ½ cup brown sugar
- 1 teaspoon vanilla extract
- 3 tablespoon milk
- 1 tablespoon Nutella
- ¼ cup almonds, chopped

Method:

1. In a large bowl, sift together the flour, baking soda, baking powder, spices and salt.
2. In another bowl, mix together the remaining ingredients except walnuts.
3. Add the banana mixture into flour mixture and mix until just combined.
4. Fold in the almonds.
5. Place the mixture into 12 greased muffin molds evenly.
6. Arrange a sheet pan in the center of Instant Omni Pro Air Fryer Oven Combo.
7. Place the muffin molds over the sheet pan.
8. Select "Air Fry" and then adjust the temperature to 248 degrees F.
9. Set the timer for 25 minutes and press "Start".
10. When the display shows "Turn Food" do nothing.

11. When cooking time is complete, remove the muffin molds from Toaster Oven and place the pan onto a wire rack for about 10 minutes.
12. Carefully, invert the muffins onto the wire rack to completely cool before serving.

Nutritional Information per Serving:

- Calories 223
- Total Fat 6.1 g
- Saturated Fat 1.5 g
- Cholesterol 45 mg
- Sodium 267 mg
- Total Carbs 38.3 g
- Fiber 2.4 g
- Sugar 15.8 g
- Protein 5 g

Pear Bread Pudding

Preparation Time: 15 minutes
Cooking Time: 44 minutes
Servings: 8

Ingredients:

For Bread Pudding:

- 10½ ounces bread, cubed
- ½ cup pear, peeled, cored and chopped
- ½ cup raisins
- ¼ cup almonds, chopped
- 1½ cups milk
- ¾ cup water
- 5 tablespoons maple syrup
- 2 teaspoons ground cinnamon
- 2 teaspoons cornstarch
- 1 teaspoon vanilla extract

For Topping:

- 1 1/3 cups plain flour
- 3/5 cup brown sugar
- 7 tablespoons butter

Method:

1. In a large bowl, mix well bread, apple, raisins, and walnuts.
2. In another bowl, add the remaining pudding ingredients and mix until well combined.
3. Add the milk mixture into bread mixture and mix until well combined.
4. Refrigerate for about 15 minutes, tossing occasionally.
5. For topping: in a bowl, mix together the flour and sugar.
6. With a pastry cutter, cut in the butter until a crumbly mixture form.

7. Place the mixture into 2 baking dishes evenly and spread the topping mixture on top of each.
8. Arrange a sheet pan in the center of Instant Omni Pro Air Fryer Oven Combo.
9. Place the 1 baking dish over the sheet pan.
10. Select "Air Fry" and then adjust the temperature to 355 degrees F.
11. Set the timer for 22 minutes and press "Start".
12. When the display shows "Turn Food" do nothing.
13. When cooking time is complete, remove the muffin molds from Toaster Oven and place the pan onto a wire rack to cool slightly.
14. Repeat with the remaining baking dish.
15. Serve warm.

Nutritional Information per Serving:

- Calories 416
- Total Fat 14 g
- Saturated Fat 7.4 g
- Cholesterol 30 mg
- Sodium 353mg
- Total Carbs 66.5 g
- Fiber 2.8 g
- Sugar 28.3 g
- Protein 7.6 g

Glazed Bananas

Preparation Time: 10 minutes
Cooking Time: 10 minutes
Servings: 2

Ingredients:

- 1 ripe banana, peeled and sliced lengthwise
- ½ teaspoon fresh lime juice
- 2 teaspoons maple syrup
- 1/8 teaspoon ground cinnamon

Method:

1. Coat each banana half with lime juice.
2. Arrange the banana halves onto the greased sheet pan, cut sides up.
3. Drizzle the banana halves with maple syrup and sprinkle with cinnamon.
4. Arrange the baking dish in the center of Instant Omni Pro Air Fryer Oven Combo.
5. Select "Air Fry" and then adjust the temperature to 350 degrees F.
6. Set the timer for 10 minutes and press the "Start".
7. When the display shows "Add Food" place the baking pan over the drip pan.
8. When the display shows "Turn Food" do nothing.
9. When cooking time is complete, remove the pan from Toaster Oven.
10. Serve immediately.

Nutritional Information per Serving:

- Calories 70
- Total Fat 0.2 g
- Saturated Fat 0.1 g
- Cholesterol 0 mg
- Sodium 1 mg
- Total Carbs 18.1 g
- Fiber 1.6 g
- Sugar 11.2 g
- Protein 0.7 g

Mini Cheesecakes

Preparation Time: 15 minutes
Cooking Time: 10 minutes
Servings: 4

Ingredients:

- ¾ cup sugar
- 2 eggs
- 1 teaspoon vanilla extract
- ½ teaspoon fresh lime juice
- 16 ounces cream cheese, softened
- 2 tablespoon heavy cream

Method:

1. In a blender, add the sugar, eggs, vanilla extract and lime juice and pulse until smooth.
2. Add the cream cheese and sour cream and pulse until smooth.
3. Place the mixture into 2 (4-inch) springform pans evenly.
4. Arrange a sheet pan in the center of Instant Omni Pro Air Fryer Oven Combo.
5. Place the ramekins over the sheet pan.
6. Select "Air Fry" and then adjust the temperature to 350 degrees F.
7. Set the timer for 10 minutes and press "Start".
8. When the display shows "Turn Food" do nothing.
9. When cooking time is complete, remove the muffin molds from Toaster Oven
10. Place the ramekins onto a wire rack to cool.
11. Refrigerate overnight before serving.

Nutritional Information per Serving:

- Calories 496
- Total Fat 31.5 g
- Saturated Fat 19.2 g
- Cholesterol 178 mg
- Sodium 486 mg
- Total Carbs 41.4 g
- Fiber 0 g
- Sugar 41.4 g
- Protein 14.2 g

Blackberries Cobbler

Preparation Time: 15 minutes
Cooking Time: 20 minutes
Servings: 6

Ingredients:

For Filling:

- 2½ cups fresh blackberries
- 1 teaspoon vanilla extract
- 1 teaspoon fresh lime juice
- 1 cup sugar
- 1 teaspoon all-purpose flour
- 1 tablespoon butter, melted

For Topping:

- 1¾ cups all-purpose flour
- 6 tablespoons sugar
- 4 teaspoons baking powder
- 1 cup milk
- 5 tablespoons butter

Method:

1. For filling: in a bowl, add all the ingredients and mix until well combined.
2. In another large bowl, mix together the flour, baking powder, and sugar.
3. Add the milk and butter and mix until a crumbly mixture form.
4. In the bottom of a greased baking dish place the blueberries mixture and top with the flour mixture evenly.
5. Arrange the baking dish in the center of Instant Omni Pro Air Fryer Oven Combo.
6. Select "Air Fry" and then adjust the temperature to 320 degrees F.
7. Set the timer for 20 minutes and press the "Start".
8. When the display shows "Add Food" place the baking pan over the drip pan.
9. When the display shows "Turn Food" do nothing.

10. When cooking time is complete, remove the pan from Toaster Oven and place onto a wire rack to cool for about 10 minutes before serving.

Nutritional Information per Serving:

- Calories 453
- Total Fat 13 g
- Saturated Fat 7.9 g
- Cholesterol 34 mg
- Sodium 105 mg
- Total Carbs 81.7 g
- Fiber 4.2 g
- Sugar 49.4 g
- Protein 6.1 g

White Chocolate Cheesecake

Preparation Time: 20 minutes
Cooking Time: 34 minutes
Servings: 6

Ingredients:

- 3 eggs (whites and yolks separated)
- 1 cup white chocolate, chopped
- ½ cup cream cheese, softened
- 2 tablespoons unsweetened cocoa powder
- 2 tablespoons powdered sugar
- ¼ cup raspberry jam

Method:

1. In a bowl, add the egg whites and refrigerate to chill before using.
2. In a microwave-safe bowl, add the chocolate and microwave on high heat for about 2 minutes, stirring after every 30 seconds.
3. In the bowl of chocolate, add the cream cheese and microwave for about 1-2 minutes or until cream cheese melts completely.
4. Remove from microwave and stir in cocoa powder and egg yolks.
5. Remove the egg whites from refrigerator and whisk until firm peaks form.
6. Add 1/3 of the mixed egg whites into cheese mixture and gently, stir to combine.
7. Fold in the remaining egg whites.
8. Place the mixture into a 6-inch cake pan.
9. Arrange a sheet pan in the center of Instant Omni Pro Air Fryer Oven Combo.
10. Place the cake pan over the sheet pan.
11. Select "Air Fry" and then adjust the temperature to 285 degrees F.
12. Set the timer for 30 minutes and press "Start".
13. When the display shows "Turn Food" do nothing.
14. When cooking time is complete, remove the muffin molds from Toaster Oven and place the pan onto a wire rack to cool completely.
15. Then, refrigerate to chill before serving.
16. Just before serving, dust with the powdered sugar.

17. Spread the jam evenly on top and serve.

Nutritional Information per Serving:

- Calories 299
- Total Fat 18.3 g
- Saturated Fat 10.6 g
- Cholesterol 109 mg
- Sodium 114 mg
- Total Carbs 29.8 g
- Fiber 0.7 g
- Sugar 25.5 g
- Protein 6.3 g

Lime Mousse

Preparation Time: 15 minutes
Cooking Time: 12 minutes
Servings: 2

Ingredients:

- 4 ounces cream cheese, softened
- ½ cup heavy cream
- 2 tablespoon fresh lime juice
- 5-6 drops liquid stevia
- Pinch of salt

Method:

1. In a bowl, add all the ingredients and mix until well combined.
2. Transfer the mixture into 2 ramekins.
3. Arrange a sheet pan in the center of Instant Omni Pro Air Fryer Oven Combo.
4. Place the ramekins over the sheet pan.
5. Select "Air Fry" and then adjust the temperature to 350 degrees F.
6. Set the timer for 12 minutes and press "Start".
7. When the display shows "Turn Food" do nothing.
8. When cooking time is complete, remove the muffin molds from Toaster Oven
9. Place the ramekins onto a wire rack to cool.
10. Refrigerate for at least 3 hours before serving.

Nutritional Information per Serving:

- Calories 302
- Total Fat 30.2 g
- Saturated Fat 19.4 g
- Cholesterol 103 mg
- Sodium 257 mg
- Total Carbs 2.4 g
- Fiber 0 g
- Sugar 0.1 g
- Protein 4.9 g

Egg Soufflé

Preparation Time: 15 minutes
Cooking Time: 30 minutes
Servings: 6

Ingredients:

- ¼ cup butter, softened
- ¼ cup all-purpose flour
- ½ cup plus 2 tablespoons sugar, divided
- 1 cup milk
- 3 teaspoons vanilla extract, divided
- 4 egg yolks
- 5 egg whites
- 1 teaspoon cream of tartar
- 2 tablespoons powdered sugar plus extra for dusting

Method:

1. In a bowl, add the butter and flour and mix until a smooth paste form.
2. In a medium pan, mix together ½ cup of sugar and milk over medium-low heat and cook for about 3 minutes or until the sugar is dissolved, stirring continuously.
3. Add the flour mixture, whisking continuously and simmer for about 3-4 minutes or until mixture becomes thick.
4. Remove from the heat and stir in 1 teaspoon of vanilla extract.
5. Set aside for about 10 minutes to cool.
6. In a bowl, mix together the egg yolks and 1 teaspoon of vanilla extract.
7. Add the egg yolk mixture into milk mixture and mix until well combined.
8. In another bowl, add the egg whites, cream of tartar, remaining sugar, and vanilla extract and whisk until stiff peaks form.
9. Fold the egg white's mixture into milk mixture.
10. Place mixture into th6 greased ramekins evenly and with the back of a spoon, smooth the top surface.
11. Arrange a sheet pan in the center of Instant Omni Pro Air Fryer Oven Combo.
12. Place the ramekins over the sheet pan.

13. Select “Air Fry” and then adjust the temperature to 330 degrees F.
14. Set the timer for 16 minutes and press “Start”.
15. When the display shows “Turn Food” do nothing.
16. When cooking time is complete, remove the muffin molds from Toaster Oven and place the pan onto a wire rack to cool slightly.
17. Sprinkle with the powdered sugar and serve warm.

Nutritional Information per Serving:

- Calories 255
- Total Fat 11.6 g
- Saturated Fat 6.5 g
- Cholesterol 163 mg
- Sodium 107mg
- Total Carbs 31.2 g
- Fiber 0.1 g
- Sugar 26.4 g
- Protein 6.8 g

Chocolate Muffins

Preparation Time: 15 minutes
Cooking Time: 10 minutes
Servings: 9

Ingredients:

- 1½ cups all-purpose flour
- ¼ cup sugar
- 2 teaspoons baking powder
- ½ teaspoon salt
- 1 cup plain Greek yogurt
- 1/3 cup olive oil
- 1 egg
- 1½ teaspoons vanilla extract
- ¼ cup semi-sweet mini chocolate chips
- ¼ cup walnuts, chopped

Method:

1. In a bowl, mix well flour, sugar, baking powder, and salt.
2. In another bowl, add the yogurt, oil, egg, and vanilla extract and whisk until well combined.
3. Add the flour mixture and mix until just combined.
4. Fold in the chocolate chips and walnuts.
5. Place the mixture into 9 greased muffin molds evenly.
6. Arrange a sheet pan in the center of Instant Omni Pro Air Fryer Oven Combo.
7. Place the muffin molds over the sheet pan.
8. Select "Air Fry" and then adjust the temperature to 355 degrees F.
9. Set the timer for 10 minutes and press "Start".
10. When the display shows "Turn Food" do nothing.
11. When cooking time is complete, remove the muffin molds from Toaster Oven and place the pan onto a wire rack for about 10 minutes.
12. Carefully, invert the muffins onto the wire rack to completely cool before serving.

Nutritional Information per Serving:

- Calories 247
- Total Fat 12.3 g
- Saturated Fat 2.8 g
- Cholesterol 20 mg
- Sodium 155 mg
- Total Carbs 28.8 g
- Fiber 0.8 g
- Sugar 11.3 g
- Protein 5.6 g

Conclusion

A healthy life begins with a scientific diet, this cookbook includes plenty of practical recipes and information about the Instant Omni Pro Air Fryer Oven Combo. I believe it will bring you a new attempt of your daily recipes. Make good use of it and start making healthier fried food. This book will become your most reliable cooking weapon. You and your family will love with the Instant Omni Pro Air Fryer Oven Combo.

What are you waiting for?

Scroll up and click Buy Now With 1-Click or Buy Now to get your copy!

CPSIA information can be obtained
at www.ICGtesting.com
Printed in the USA
BVHW060741230721
612634BV00003B/442